M000209220

PIGEONS

Contents

Photography: Herbert R. Axelrod, 20 bottom. Charles Heitzman, 80 top. Lilo Hess, 63. Ho Yan Ning, 74 top. Hutton, 74 bottom. R. L. Kienlen (courtesy of Ralston Purina Company), 14, 15, 18, 67, 71, 75. Gordon L'Allemand, 61, 62, 68. Michelin Animal Photography, 58. Carl Naether, 55. George Neuerburg, 23. B. Pawlik, 57. Scheide (courtesy of Schutte), 31 bottom. Stauber, 19, 22, 66 bottom. Lucille Stewart, 8. Courtesy of Three Lions, 39, 47, 49, 72. U. S. Army Air Forces, McChord Field, Washington, 73. U. S. Army Signal Corps, 88. Louise Van der Meid, front and back endpapers, 6, 7, 10, 11, 13, 26, 27, 29, 32, 38, 41, 42, 44, 45, 46, 52, 56, 65, 70, 78, 79, 81, 83, 86, 87 top, 90, 91. Courtesy of Vogelpark Walsrode, 54. Don White, 28, 34.

Many of the Racing Homers shown here are owned by Doug and Linda Darst of Salem, Oregon.

Distributed in the UNITED STATES by T.F.H. Publications, Inc., 211 West Sylvania Avenue, Neptune City, NJ 07753; in CANADA by H & L Pet Supplies Inc., 27 Kingston Crescent, Kitchener, Ontario N2B 2T6; Rolf C. Hagen Ltd., 3225 Sartelon Street, Montreal 382 Quebec; in ENGLAND by T.F.H. Publications Limited, 4 Kier Park, Ascot, Berkshire SL5 7DS; in AUSTRALIA AND THE SOUTH PACIFIC by T.F.H. (Australia) Pty. Ltd., Box 149, Brookvale 2100 N.S.W., Australia; in NEW ZEALAND by Ross Haines & Son, Ltd., 18 Monmouth Street, Grey Lynn, Auckland 2 New Zealand; in SINGAPORE AND MALAYSIA by MPH Distributors Pte., 71-77 Stamford Road, Singapore 0617; in the PHILIPPINES by Bio-Research, 5 Lippay Street, San Lorenzo Village, Makati Rizal; in SOUTH AFRICA by Multipet Pty. Ltd., 30 Turners Avenue, Durban 4001. Published by T.F.H. Publications Inc., Ltd. the British Crown Colony of Hong Kong.

PIGEONS

Carl Naether

Pigeons *(left)* have been domesticated for thousands of years. Among those domestic pigeons that continue to fascinate us today are the racing breeds *(below)* that are trained for competition.

Introduction

The purpose of this book is to introduce you to the various pleasures of keeping pigeons, on the assumption that you have not engaged in this fascinating hobby before. Domestic breeds of pigeons fall into three general groups: so-called fancy pigeons, racing pigeons, and utility (squabbing) pigeons. Fancy pigeons, which usually include the tumbling and the high-flying varieties, are raised mainly for exhibition and prize-winning in local and national shows. Racing, or homing, pigeons are kept principally for competitive flying in races staged by local and state racing-pigeon clubs. In these races, speed and distance are the main governing factors which decide winning entries. Finally, utility pigeons are kept for the purpose of raising squabs, either in small numbers for the keeper's own table, or in large numbers for the commercial market; in other words, for profit. Of course, all

Swiss Mondaine, a breed that is especially suited to squab production.

varieties of domestic pigeons produce edible squabs. Thus, the offspring of fancy and of racing pigeons which do not, for one reason or another, meet the required exhibition or racing standards and therefore do not justify their keeping and breeding, usually "go into the pot."

Pigeon keeping is a delightful, educational activity for young and old alike. In this hobby, you deal with lovely, live birds which you can easily tame, and whose life cycle, from the eggs to the full-grown birds, you can observe at close range day in and day out. This affords you an excellent opportunity to learn at firsthand how one of the most popular domesticated creatures propagates and maintains its kind. Moreover, there are several hundred varieties of domesticated pigeons. Some, such as the Modenas, Oriental Frills, Starlings, and Swallows, are kept mainly for the handsome coloring of their plumage; some, such as the Pouters, Magpies, Maltese, Show Homers, and many others, are valued for their odd shapes and postures; some, such as the Rollers and Tipplers delight their keepers with aerial tumbling and long-time high-flying. It is perhaps no exaggeration to assert that one can get, for his own pigeon-raising hobby, birds of so many different shapes and sizes, as to please even the most discriminating taste. Especially is this the case today when there exists a lively "flight" of European breeds to this country, which the increasing use of air-freight has made possible. The result of this increasing influx of breeds often little known in this country has been to greatly enrich and enhance our American pigeon shows, and in consequence to induce American pigeon men and women to try their hand at breeding and perfecting the imported specimens.

Unquestionably, the general prosperity existing in America at this writing and a noticeable increase in leisure time are in no small part responsible for the fast-growing popularity which pigeon keeping as a pastime enjoys today. This popularity is reflected in the ever-growing memberships of local and national pigeon clubs and associations, which are responsible for staging lively shows each year. These are get-together occasions where enthusiastic pigeon men and women find out how well their own birds compare with the best in the land, and where they often form life-long friendships with persons of like minds and interests.

CARL NAETHER

Pigeon keeping can be done on a small scale *(left)* with a single bird or a pair kept in a cage, or it can develop into a more elaborate hobby *(below)* with many breeding pairs housed in a loft.

Keeping Pigeons for Pleasure and for Profit

Perhaps you will agree that in order to make the keeping of any kind of livestock truly pleasurable, tameness is essential. Certainly, this quality applies to keeping domestic pigeons, for if they are handled with patience and consideration, if they are not chased about and roughly handled, but are treated quietly and gently, they will quickly become tame and trusting. Truly tame pigeons are a delight to keep and to breed. You can enter their loft, and instead of shying and flying away from you as if you were their enemy, they will remain quiet, attending to their nests and young; or, if it happens to be their feeding time, they will flock to you, eagerly accepting the offered food. In other words, they regard you as their friend and benefactor. This tameness is especially convenient when you go into the loft to inspect the nests of your pigeons to learn which settings of eggs have

hatched, which pair of youngsters is old enough to be banded, and in general to make sure that the breeding activities of each pair are making noticeable progress.

If, perchance, you have bought pigeons which are shy and easily frightened as you approach them, it usually means that they have been maltreated by their former keeper. By treating them quietly and gently, however, and making no sudden, quick movements while you are in their loft, you can gradually tame them.

If you want them to take feed from your hand, stand stock-still, and throw some kernels a short distance on the floor of the pen where the birds will come and get them. Then narrow this distance from day to day, until, finally, you drop the feed at your feet or place it in the open palm of your hand, holding it perfectly still. This desirable tameness of your pigeons is not only very convenient in the loft, but also in the show pen at judging time, for there the truly tame pigeon will display its best qualities much more readily and quickly than the frightened one. An exhibitor can hardly blame a judge at a show for paying extra attention to the pigeon he can easily take in hand to appraise its qualities.

Breeding for color is another fascination of the pigeon fancier, since many breeds score a good many points in the official standard if they possess what are usually called correct markings, or in the case of one-color breeds, that *one* color as prescribed by the standard. Since there are literally hundreds of different, and often very beautiful, color combinations in domestic pigeons, there is truly no end to breeding so-called color pigeons to meet official breed standards. Or, if the pigeon enthusiast is inclined to "create" new color combinations, he can easily obtain the necessary material.

Breeding beautifully colored pigeons which will please not only the eye of their owner, but also that of the judge in the show hall, may be considered both an art and a

The more time one spends with his pigeons, the more likely the birds are to become hand-tame. Move slowly, talk softly, and by all means be gentle in your approach.

Two interesting characteristics of the Norwich Cropper, a breed of pouter pigeon, are its inflated globe and its erect carriage.

This colorful English Short-faced Tumbler, a red mottled agate hen, has a similarly erect stance and is clean-legged like the Norwich Cropper; however, it is a smaller bird with shorter legs and a very rounded breast.

science, for it usually requires an artist to "create" and to evaluate colors in pigeons, and a scientist to learn and apply the genetic principles underlying color breeding. Unless the pigeon hobbyist knows how to apply these principles effectively, he is not likely to succeed in breeding his birds to the desired color schemes with any degree of exactness. Well-planned, judicious breeding of pigeons for color is unquestionably one of the most absorbing and rewarding aspects of raising pigeons as a hobby. A large number of European breeds, many of which are now also fairly common in this country, such as Shields, Crescents, Suabians, Starlings, Swallows, Ice Pigeons, Larks, and numerous others, boast unique and very pleasing color markings in such wide variety that the hobbyist can select those particular color combinations which please him most. To breed any single one of these varieties to perfection, or true to the standard so far as color is concerned, is a joyous task likely to provide the pigeon keeper with almost endless hours of absorbing interest year in and year out.

A third, no less inviting aspect of pigeon keeping is breeding for the right size, shape, stature, and appendage, as set by the standard. So-called *form* pigeons, some of which, such as the Magpie, the various Croppers and Pouters, the Show Homer, Scandaroon, Stargard Swanneck, and others enjoying considerable popularity in pigeondom, are bred principally for the conformation prescribed by the official breed standard. While the shape and figure of these breeds may appear to be rather odd and even somewhat artificial to the novice, to the breed enthusiast they are, to say the least, eminently handsome and certainly worth perpetuating by means of careful pairing. Some of the form pigeons, such as the Magpie and the Show Homer, have reached such a high degree of perfection of body conformation, etc., that further improvement is most likely to be achieved only by a long-experienced, patient, and very conscientious fancier. To a novice, such breeds are likely to bring disappointment for the simple reason that very often years of intelligent effort are required to show noticeable improvement in a Show Homer, a Carrier, a Maltese, or a Magpie. Only dyed-in-the-wool fanciers should occupy their time and talent with such and similar classic breeds.

A further and very enjoyable feature of the pigeon-raising hobby, particularly suited to youngsters and to beginners in general, is to keep tumbling and flying breeds, including so-called Tumblers, Rollers, Tipplers, Swing Pouters, and others. The indispensable requirement here is that the hobbyist live in a community where no serious objections are likely to be voiced against pigeons alighting on neighboring housetops. With a small kit of a dozen or so well-trained and well-performing Tumblers, usually called Rollers, a youngster, or an oldster, can have many hours of fun in the open air, watching the aerial antics which his birds perform. By a whistling or a rattling of the feed can they'll return to the loft, to be fed and kept until time for the next fly approaches. Roller pigeons occur in so many different colors that choice of any one or of several is rarely difficult. Moreover, these pigeons are easy to keep because they are dependable feeders and fast breeders, thus enabling the novice to assemble within a short time an ample number for one or more sizeable kits. In point of fact, Rollers are such conscientious parents that they are often utilized as "feeders" for the young of breeds which for one reason or another do not or cannot raise their own squabs. Since they are kept by many fanciers in considerable numbers, Roller pigeons, always quite popular with young and old, are usually moderately priced.

A wholly different pleasure is provided by another breed of flying pigeons: Tipplers. These rather dainty little beauties are kept for long-time high flying. Thus a

Three fancy pigeon breeds: Crested Helmet *(above)*; Franconian Velvet-Shield *(facing page, above)*, known for its glossy plumage; Black Scandaroon *(facing page, below)*, with its unusually-shaped beak.

A pair of one-year-old almond English Short-faced Tumblers.

Yellow plain-headed American Domestic Flight.

kit of Tipplers will soar high above the clouds, there to fly in graceful circles for hours on end. At times, these wonderful endurance flyers remain so long in the air that they are overtaken by nightfall and thus lost to their keeper. They ascend so high in the heavens that they become mere specks to their observer. Various clubs of Tippler fanciers stage many competitions annually—flights of well-trained kits whose quality is judged mainly by the number of hours they remain aloft. To bring his kit of Tipplers into the best possible condition for endurance flights, the keeper adheres to a strict routine of exercise and careful and special feeding, all designed to maintain his birds in fine fettle. Flying Tipplers is a sport of absorbing interest because the sportsman's admiration for his wonderful little performers grows with each new season.

Finally, I come to that feature of pigeoneering which appeals to thousands of young and not-so-young Americans: pigeon racing. It is based on what is termed the homing instinct: the insistent urge in the pigeon, when it finds itself in strange surroundings, to fly off and return to its familiar home loft as quickly as possible.

The sport of racing pigeons is practiced or indulged in, in every civilized country. Apparently guided by the light of the sun, pigeons, when properly trained, will find their home in due time even though released in strange surroundings and even though compelled to fly over unfamiliar territory. Hundreds upon hundreds of racing-pigeon clubs are living proof of the tremendous hold which this fine sport has on thousands of intelligent men and women in this country. It takes an intelligent fancier to succeed as a pigeon racer, because training of both young and old birds, for the short as well as for the long-distance races, has to be very carefully planned and executed regularly. The racing-pigeon fancier must study the requirements of each one of his racers, since no

Many pigeons are attractively marked, as is the case with the silver-barred English Show Homer *(above)*, the Checkered Ice Pigeon *(facing page, above)*, and the Barred Starling *(facing page, below)*.

two birds are alike in the manner in which they fly in races and in which they respond to training. Only to the extent to which he knows each bird's ability is he likely to succeed in the strongly competitive races featured by clubs in every part of this country.

There are both junior and senior racing-pigeon clubs, with well-organized and well-informed memberships. These clubs establish their own sets of rules for racing, the number of young-bird and old-bird races to be flown each season, and the distances as well as the directions in which the birds are to fly. Membership in a racing-pigeon club usually means that the pigeoneer has sufficient financial means to purchase excellent racing stock, materials for a modern loft, and whatever else is needed to enable him to compete on fairly even terms with the other club members.

Racing, or homing, pigeons come in a wide variety of colors, with the more modest ones, such as the blue-bar, blue-check, red, red-check, etc., being much more common than light colors, such as white, yellow, or mealy, which are often more easily spotted by birds of prey than are the darker colors. Their requisite qualities are physical stamina and mental alertness, in addition, of course, to a well-developed homing instinct. Probably the best strains of Racing Homers have come to America from Belgium, where pigeon racing is a *national* pastime, with thousands of dollars to be won on national race days when thousands of homers darken the skies over this little European land. England also has supplied American fanciers with some excellent stock.

In order to succeed with racing pigeons, one should purchase the best possible foundation stock from a fancier well known for his recent winnings in races, both short and long distance. Some strains of racing pigeons fly best in short (100–300 mile) races, while other strains fly best in the long (500–1000 mile) races. By *strain* is meant a family of pigeons which is of the same bloodline, and which has been developed by inbreeding, such as mating closely-related birds, avoiding the introduction of any new, "outside" blood (which is usually referred to as *outcrossing*). Years of concentrated, intelligent effort are required to produce a successful strain of racing pigeons; hence, the usually high prices asked, and obtained, for such quality stock. Absolutely nothing is achieved with mediocre racing pigeons, that is, if one plans to enter his birds in club competition. More novice fanciers of this wonderfully stimulating sport have been lost to the racing-pigeon fancy by using shoddy foundation stock than by any other means. It pays to start with the very best foundation stock one can afford. Needless to say, the demands on the fancier's intelligence and character, as well as on his time and pocketbook, are such as to make it inadvisable for anyone not possessing these qualities and means to join the ranks of racing-pigeon men and women.

Now that I have sketched for you the principal features which combine to make pigeon keeping such a delightful and educational pastime, you will, I trust, be better able to judge which particular phase of this popular hobby is most likely to appeal to you individually, in harmony with your personal likes and dislikes, with your financial means, and with the physical surroundings likely to lend themselves to a loft location.

During the breeding season, mated pairs should be furnished with at least two nest pans and suitable nesting materials *(left)*. Racing Homers *(below)* need special quarters, which include traps to catch returning birds.

*Housing
Pigeons
Properly*

To keep pigeons in good health and breeding condition you do not need any elaborate equipment or expensive buildings. They will feel at home in almost any enclosure, provided that it is brightly lit, draft-proof, water-proof, and vermin-proof. Most domestic pigeons are kept in lofts which consist of two parts: a solid, roofed-over, so-called permanent shelter, and, attached to it, a wired-in flight. The shelter, or house, contains the nest boxes, usually set in tiers against the back wall. It serves as the pigeons' roosting and breeding place. The flight, covered on top, on the sides, and on the front with half-inch wire mesh, is the birds' exercise and relaxation quarters. Here they can fly about to their hearts' content, bask in the sunshine, bathe, and in general follow their individual, natural inclinations. The flight is usually equipped with some smooth perching, or alighting, boards placed three

Some pigeon lofts consist of a permanent shelter to which a porch is attached. The wired-in enclosure allows the birds to sun themselves and enjoy fresh air.

or four feet off the ground along the sides so as to leave as much space as possible in the center for unhindered flying. Depending on climatic and other conditions, feed containers, grit boxes, and drinkers, all suitably covered to prevent soiling, are set in either the flight or the shelter.

The size of both the shelter and the flight varies with the number and the varieties of pigeons kept. It should always be sufficiently roomy to avoid crowding. It is ever so much more satisfactory, both from the fancier's and the birds' standpoint, to keep a limited number of breeding pairs in ample space. Here they can easily get out of the way of one another and do not have to fight incessantly for roosting or breeding accommodations, as is the case in close quarters. Crowding is bound to result in fights over the possession of nest sites, with resulting damage to eggs and injury to squabs. Far more than any other single cause, crowding of pigeons is responsible for much so-called bad luck in the loft. This can easily be

Many breeders who feed their pigeons by hand adhere to a regular feeding schedule: food is offered once in the morning and again in the afternoon.

Pigeons picking at grit on the floor of the shelter entrance *(above)*. White domestic pigeons *(facing page);* the specimen below is a utility pigeon.

Incubating eggs and brooding young are duties shared by both cock and hen *(above)*. Nest boxes can be set up in tiers in a breeding loft *(below)*.

avoided if the keeper will exercise self-control and not put more birds in his loft than it was meant to accommodate when he built it.

Under ordinary conditions, it is good practice to provide about one cubic foot of nest box space for each pair of breeders. Being quite prolific, most pairs will have young and eggs frequently at just about the same time; that is, when the squabs are several weeks old, the hen will be laying her second clutch of eggs. For this, she must have a second nest box, preferably adjoining the first one. To prevent pairs fighting for nesting accommodations, it is good policy to place more nest boxes in the loft than there are breeding pairs. The minimum is two for each pair of birds. The boxes may be fastened on the back wall of the shelter, where the sunlight can bring warmth and light to them for part of the day, and where the fancier can watch the nesting activities of his birds from the outside, without having to enter the loft.

Inexpensive yet useful nest sites may be made from open-top wooden boxes. With their bottoms set against, or fastened to, the back wall of the shelter, the boxes are set in tiers, their open fronts having a six-inch board nailed across the bottom to prevent young squabs from falling out in case they leave the nest bowl. Each box should have a solid roof to prevent the nest from being soiled by birds perching on top of the box. Perches in front of the nest boxes are not needed, since the pigeons will fly directly onto and into the nest sites. Moreover, such perches would only encourage fighting. A nest bowl, or nest pan, made of a material heavy enough so that the pigeons cannot upset it, is placed in each box. Such bowls are obtainable at animal-supply stores, which, incidentally, also stock all sorts of feeders, drinkers, and other loft accessories.

Some fanciers like to place a pinch of Black-Leaf Forty (an insecticide) in the bottom of each nest pan to keep

These small wooden buildings, equipped with feed hoppers, screened-in porches, and water pans, are suitable pigeon enclosures.

lice and mites away, then fill the pan partly with clean sand, short-cut hay, or other nesting material. Being rather poor nest builders, the pigeons will readily accept this help from their keeper. In some lofts, you will find racks stuffed with tobacco stems on the floor of the loft, which the pigeons pull out stem by stem and carry to their nests. The pungent odor of tobacco stems is said to keep mites and lice away from the nests. When the squabs have left the nest, near the age of four weeks, the pans are then best taken out and thoroughly cleaned.

Heavy breeds of pigeons, such as Runts, which fly but little, and other breeds which stay on the floor of the loft most of the time, should be given nest boxes on the ground. Naturally, the size of the box should be suited to the size of the pigeons it is meant to accommodate. When it becomes desirable to exercise strict control over the breeding activities of each pair, as, for example, in Racing Homer lofts, each breeding compartment, consisting of two nest sites, has a wire front equipped with a door, which can be locked. In such a compartment individual pairs are usually caged until they have laid eggs. These wire fronts are carried in stock by pigeon-supply houses.

Lacking perhaps sufficient financial means to erect sizeable lofts, novice pigeon keepers often find it needful to utilize attics, garden sheds, as well as unused parts of barns as lofts for their birds. These should be light, dry, and accessible. A rather common drawback of such facilities is that they are not vermin-proof. Mice and rats are quickly attracted to places where grain is fed to livestock. If they gain access to pigeon lofts, they will, especially during the night, disturb birds sitting on eggs or young. Rats have been known to attack and injure squabs in the nest. Unless such lofts can be made mouse- and rat-proof, they are of little practical use.

Being hardy, domestic pigeons can endure considerable heat and cold, provided that they are well fed and not needlessly exposed to extreme temperatures for long periods of time, and can retreat into a solidly covered, draft-proof, dry shelter whenever they wish. The front of this shelter should be so located as to admit the morning sun. In mild climates, the front is kept open the year 'round; in other climates, the front may be made of wood, with windows and a door, which are usually left open during pleasant weather. Carefully designed permanent shelters are often equipped with special windows, ventilators, and electric lighting—expensive and not always necessary items which the novice may wish to forego, at least for a time.

While pigeons are quite hardy, they do not like to stand or sit on a cold, damp, or wet floor. The floor should be kept dry, if at all possible. It may consist of natural soil, wood, or concrete, and is best covered with a six-inch layer of clean sand, which should be periodically raked and renewed. In the flight portion of the loft, good drainage should be provided to prevent rainwater or snow-water from standing in puddles, which the birds soon dirty and from which they often drink.

Burrowing animals, such as mice and rats, may be kept out of the loft by sinking a concrete foundation about eighteen inches into the ground around the entire structure, setting both shelter and flight supports on it. Quarter-inch wire netting tacked to the top, sides, and front of the flight will keep mice, rats, etc., from getting into it. A vermin-free loft tends to keep its occupants healthy and free to follow their natural inclinations. The extra cost occasioned by vermin-proofing a pigeon loft is practical assurance of the pigeons' general well-being and uninterrupted breeding. Moreover, there is not a fancier living who does not keenly enjoy working in a vermin-free loft, where he does not have to bother constantly with setting traps or putting out poison for undesirable "guests."

The walls of the loft are best whitewashed at least once a year to keep them both attractive and reasonably clean. Nest boxes, perches, and other furnishings should be thoroughly washed and disinfected at the close of the breeding season so as to be ready for use the following spring. Racing-pigeon men and women are most painstaking in keeping their lofts free from dirt. If keepers of fancy and utility pigeons followed this example, they would derive more satisfaction from their hobby, and their birds would be cleaner and healthier.

Lofts designed for Racing Homers are usually furnished with special equipment, such as traps for catching birds returning from races; individual breeding compartments with cage fronts; electric lighting, both inside and outside of the loft; running water for drinking and bathing; individual, V-shaped perches; and other similar facilities. These lofts are usually located so that the birds from within the loft, through the windows of the traps, get a panoramic view of the surrounding countryside. This is one good reason why racing lofts are frequently situated on high ground.

Utility (squabbing) pigeons are kept in so-called battery cages, which are quite similar to chicken batteries. Equipped with feeders, drinkers, and grit containers, as well as with wire bottoms, these cages accommodate one breeding pair each with its two nests. Kept purely for squab production, the birds have no flying or other exercise room in the cage, where their breeding activities are easily inspected and controlled. Such cage keeping of pigeons lacks humaneness and is not particularly recommended.

In building any kind of substantial, more or less permanent pigeon house, the novice should acquaint himself with the nature and the structure of lofts found in his neighborhood, since these have in most cases been adapted to climatic and other important local conditions affecting the welfare of pigeons. He can, therefore, get sound, practical ideas by visiting neighborhood lofts. Moreover, by carefully noting other fanciers' facilities, the novice will see at firsthand and in actual use various loft accessories, such as feeders, drinkers, bath pans, nest bowls, perches, and whatever else is needed to keep pigeons in vigorous health and breeding condition. Finally, it will pay him to visit local animal-supply houses and look over the loft accessories they may have to offer pigeon fanciers.

Tame pigeons, after a bit of persuasion, may allow their keeper to feed them by hand when they go to nest *(left)*. Homemade or packaged feed mixtures can be offered *(below)*.

Feeding and Caring for Pigeons

Feeding domestic pigeons is a simple matter. Being grain eaters, they thrive on a mixture of whole corn, peas, milo, and wheat. These grains may be given them in one mixture, which is usually called pigeon feed, and is available throughout the United States. For Racing Homers, a special mixture containing more peas than the ordinary mixture is available.

The mixture is given the birds in hoppers, into which they cannot step and thus dirty the feed. After twenty or thirty minutes, depending on the number of pigeons feeding, the number of squabs in the nest, and the season of the year, the hoppers are removed, the birds having supposedly satisfied their hunger. If perchance they have left much feed in the hoppers, it indicates that they are being overfed; then the quantity should be reduced. Of course, when pigeons are feeding squabs in the nests,

they require heavier feeding.

In some lofts you will find feed hoppers having a separate compartment for each kind of grain, and also one for grit and one for mineral supplements. These so-called cafeteria feeders may hold from a few to many pounds of grain; and, depending on their capacity, they may need replenishing only once a week or once a month. Their use means, of course, that the birds can help themselves to the feed and grit at any time of day, and also that they can "make their own mixtures," selecting for this purpose the various grains in such quantities as their instinct tells them they, as well as their youngsters, need. Most cafeteria feeders are equipped with glass fronts which enable the fancier to tell at any time just how much of each kind of grain and grit is left in each compartment and also which kinds of grain his birds prefer at given seasons of the year and at various stages in their breeding activities. The novice should keep in mind that pigeons, properly cared for, do not overeat; consequently, keeping feed before them all day long harms them in no way. Unquestionably, the use of cafeteria feeders saves much time and effort, particularly in lofts housing large numbers of pigeons.

On the other hand, many a beginner greatly enjoys feeding his birds by hand twice a day: fairly early in the morning and in the middle of the afternoon. Such feeding affords him a splendid opportunity to make friends with his birds and to tame them. He should, of course, feed regularly, at the same times each day, so that the birds will form the habit of looking for their friend and keeper morning and afternoon, eagerly flying to him when he comes into their loft with the feed can. Irregular or haphazard feeding is bad for pigeons, as it is for most livestock, since it seriously retards the growth and development of the young in the nests. If, therefore, the novice cannot attend to the twice-a-day feeding schedule day in

Some breeders prefer to feed their birds in a trough instead of scattering grain on the floor of the loft where it will become soiled.

Feeding pigeons by hand is a sure way of taming the birds; in time, they come to recognize and trust their keeper's gentle hand.

and day out, he should use self-feeders, as described above, thus keeping feed before his birds all the time.

While most pigeon keepers feed grains to their birds, quite a few are trying out the so-called pigeon pellets which contain all the necessary food elements, as well as minerals. Naturally the use of pellets simplifies the task of feeding pigeons even more than does the self-feeder with its various compartments. For Racing Homers a special pellet is offered by some supply houses.

Fresh, clean drinking water, kept cool in summer and free of ice in winter, is essential to the pigeons' health. If it is given to them in shallow, galvanized, open pans, where it often gets stale, it should be replaced at least once a day and the pans rinsed out at the same time. The pans should be so covered as to prevent the water from being soiled by birds perching directly above them. To keep them from stepping into the drinking water, round wire guards fitting the pans are effective. In well-equipped lofts, automatic watering devices and fountains are in use. They release water sufficient only to keep it at a certain level, thus serving the birds with fresh, cool water all day long. In regions subject to severe winters, automatic drinkers tend to freeze up and thus to give trouble.

All pigeons naturally love to bathe and to keep their feathers clean and shining. Once or twice a week, summer and winter, the novice should place on the floor of the flight wide, shallow pans filled with water just deep enough for the birds to stand (not to float!) in. When the birds have finished bathing, the water should be taken away to keep them from drinking it. Following their bath, they will preen their plumage for quite some time, greatly enjoying themselves.

The beak on a pigeon nestling *(left)* is formed in such a way that it can be inserted into the parents' mouths at feeding time. A pair diligently watch over their brood *(below)*.

Breeding Pigeons

For the novice, by far the most satisfactory way to get started with pigeons is to buy one or more pairs of *mated* birds. Most likely, after they have been a week or ten days in their new surroundings and well cared for there, they will begin to "work" for him; that is, they will lay eggs and raise young. Pigeons usually mate for life, rearing squabs season after season, often for ten years or even longer.

Sexing the birds is important. The male pigeon, or cock, is usually larger than the hen. He has a thicker neck and larger head, is much more aggressive, and his neck feathers are often more brightly colored than those of the hen. A sure characteristic of the male pigeon is his frequent habit of cooing and of strutting about. He will court another pigeon with loud, enthusiastic coos. Moreover, with air-inflated crop and spreading tail, he will boldly bear down on the other bird, all the while "danc-

Hen pigeons do most of the feeding for the first few weeks; later the cock offers assistance.

ing" about and scraping the ground with his tail. During nest building, he is the one that carries twigs and straws to the chosen site, giving them to the hen. Sitting in the nest bowl, she arranges these materials 'round about herself. To recognize male pigeons quickly in their lofts, some pigeon fanciers place either numbered or brightly-colored bands on their right legs, while they band the hens on the left legs.

Billing and lovemaking in general is a sure sign of mating. The female inserts her beak into the open beak of the male, who then regurgitates some food. Usually billing is followed by mating, the male treading the squatting female. After the mating ceremony, the male indulges in a short, joyous flight, in which he is usually followed by his mate. This nuptial flight is engaged in particularly by pigeons which are kept in roomy flights or which have liberty outside of their lofts.

Mated pairs are generally most productive if cock and

Once a nest site is accepted, the cock begins to carry nesting materials to his mate.

hen are of decidedly different ages. Thus, a cock two or more years old mated to a year-old hen is more likely to produce fertile eggs and to raise vigorous offspring than a pair consisting of, say, a three-year-old cock and hen, or of one-year-old birds. Furthermore, mating a young bird to an older bird often means more successful nesting, since the latter is already experienced in nest building, incubating, and the feeding of squabs.

A healthy, mated pair of pigeons, placed in a new loft, will, after a few days of getting acquainted with their strange environment, begin to look for a suitable place to nest. In this activity, the cock bird takes the initiative by inspecting nest boxes in various locations. As soon as he has found one to his liking, he will stay in it, loudly calling to his mate to come and have a look at the prospective home. If she shows approval of the site—by readily entering it and for some time staying in it with her mate—then he will soon start to carry nesting materials to her. These she fixes 'round about her in the nest bowl, all the while turning and twisting. Most pigeons build flimsy nests, which is a good reason why some fanciers fill the nest pans partly with clean sand or other suitable foundation material, on top of which the birds can then lay their loose structures of twigs and stems.

At this particular stage of the breeding activities (that is, before the eggs are laid), the cock may be seen *driving* his mate to the nest. He chases her about the loft, often vigorously pecking at her, and gives her barely enough time to eat and to drink. This driving stops as soon as she has laid the first egg, which usually happens in the afternoon. While the hen is on the nest, her mate often continues to gather twigs and straws, eagerly carrying them to her. After a day's interval, the hen drops the second egg. Then incubation, lasting from seventeen to nineteen days (its exact duration varying with climatic and other conditions), begins in earnest. Both birds share in brood-

48

When eggs are first laid, they are creamy white. Incubation begins immediately and lasts for approximately seventeen to nineteen days.

ing the eggs, the cock sitting from about ten o'clock in the forenoon until about four o'clock in the afternoon, and the hen the remaining time of day and night.

While incubating and, indeed, during all their nesting activities, most pigeons will defend their nests vigorously against all intruders, human and others. They will peck at them repeatedly and flap their wings at them, uttering sharp, short coos. If the novice has tamed his birds thoroughly, they will usually, though of course reluctantly, let him inspect their nests without raising too much fuss; but if his pigeons are shy and wild, they are likely to leave their nests hurriedly at his interference, at times breaking eggs or dragging young out of their nests. Frequent nest inspections, which are more or less undesirable interference with the birds' natural breeding functions, should be avoided at all costs, as should repeated handling of young squabs.

When first laid, the eggs of domestic pigeons are glossy white; after about a week's steady incubation they turn a bluish gray. This darkening of their color is a sure sign of fertility. When the squabs have hatched, the old birds will carry the empty eggshells, which might otherwise smother the young birds, out of the nest. Now the parents will take regular turns at brooding their offspring day and night for a week or ten days, keeping them sufficiently warm and generally protecting them. Some pairs will brood their young for but a few days, thus running the risk of losing the almost-naked, blind squabs on cold days or cold nights.

Pigeons feed their young by means of regurgitation, with the latter inserting their tender little beaks between those of their elders, who then literally pump a soft, mushy substance, called pigeon milk, into the squabs' crops. As the youngsters grow, their crops receive less and less soft food and more small grains until, at approximately three weeks of age, they are quite ready to digest the hard and often quite large grains which their parents eat. Most pigeons feed their young shortly after they themselves have eaten and drunk. They will fill their crops with various available grains, then take some grit, and finally hasten to the waterpans, freely drinking a considerable quantity of water with which to soften the hard grains in their crops. Now that the meal for the youngsters is ready and complete, they will fly to the nest, there to regurgitate the watery mixture.

When the squabs are very young, the hen does most of the feeding. Later on, when they are two or three weeks old, at which time she gets ready to start another nest, the cock assumes the feeding of the squabs. This he continues until, at the age of six or seven weeks, when they have been out of the nest for ten or more days, they become self-dependent.

Some breeds of pigeons, such as Homers, Tumblers,

Rollers, and others, are known as eager and dependable feeders of their young. For this reason, they often serve as foster parents for the young of other breeds which, for one reason or another, do not or cannot feed their young very well. There are also considerable differences between individual pairs of pigeons so far as their habits of feeding their offspring regularly and thoroughly is concerned. Of course, all pigeons rearing young should have access to a plentiful supply of feed, grit, and water, both for themselves and their young.

If squabs are fed poorly, they are likely to jump out of their nests sooner than those that are fed well and regularly, for the latter are more content to remain where they are. Usually, however, young pigeons will leave the nest when they are approximately a month old, still being fed by their male parent for a week or ten days. When out of the nest and running about on the floor of the loft, the youngsters, seeing other pigeons peck at the food or plunge their beaks into the drinking water, soon begin to imitate them. And it is certainly not long before they themselves eat and drink, especially since their parents, now having a new nest to attend to, don't feed them as often. As soon as the young are wholly self-supporting, they should be removed to other quarters so that they will not interfere in any way with the activities of the breeding pairs. This suggests a very important aspect of pigeon keeping: namely, how to keep mated pairs in a state of steady, more or less uninterrupted breeding.

To keep peace among his mated pairs, the novice, or for that matter any pigeon keeper, should under no condition tolerate any unmated cocks or hens in his breeding loft. Such extra birds will invariably keep the settled pairs in constant turmoil and trouble, for they will try to mate with already-paired birds, often forcing their way into their nests, where nasty fighting causes broken eggs and injured young. Single males or females have no place whatsoever in a breeding loft: they should either be kept separately or else be disposed of. If the novice wants his family of pigeons to be orderly and thriving, then he should keep *only mated pairs* in all his breeding pens. If he wants to add a new pair to such a pen, the best way to settle these birds is to *cage* them for a week or so in a vacant nesting compartment until they have laid eggs, for then he can be reasonably certain that these newcomers will not try to take over already-occupied nest boxes by vicious fighting. It cannot be emphasized too strongly or too often that the two most common and most serious causes of failure in pigeon raising, committed especially by beginners, are keeping extra cocks or hens, or both, with already-mated pairs; and crowding more and more birds into limited space, with little or no regard for the comfort and the health of the flock as a whole.

Now for some pertinent comments on so-called methods of breeding. If the novice aims at breeding pigeons fit for show competition, he should buy one or more mated pairs of high-quality birds from a reputable fancier, one who has bred his variety for many years, during which time he has achieved notable winnings on the show bench. Such a fancier has practiced, for a very considerable period of time, both inbreeding and linebreeding; that is, when he started, he took a certain number of birds, very carefully analyzed their strong as well as their weak features in the light of the official breed standard, and then mated cocks and hens so that their offspring would (so he hoped and prayed!) possess the strong features of *both* in larger measure and their weak features in lesser measure. From this offspring, in turn, he would very carefully select, again in the light of the breed standard, the very best birds for mating, continuing this procedure year after year without introducing any new or foreign blood into his family (strain, or line) of birds.

Inbreeding usually means pairing closely related members of a family, such as father to daughter, mother to son, etc., the purpose being intensification of certain desirable qualities, such as color, shape, weight, etc., but without intensification of undesirable qualities. If pigeons so bred are in sound health and if they are cared for efficiently, they are not likely to produce weak youngsters, though infertile eggs must at times be expected. Linebreeding simply means developing a line, or distinct family, of birds and is usually accomplished by pairing not-too-closely related birds. In other words, it is a form of less intensive inbreeding.

When a fancier buys birds from another loft to pair with his own, for the purpose of improving his own strain, he is said to use the method of crossing, or outcrossing. With this new blood, he will introduce into his strain not only its good, but also its bad features, which, being subject to inheritance from previous generations, are often not visible at the time of purchase. Outcrossing, in other words, occasions much risk, since if a given hidden bad quality possessed by the newly-introduced birds crops up prominently in the offspring, it may require generations of painstaking breeding to eliminate it. Many a well-intentioned novice, having been taken by an especially fine specimen at a show, has bought this prizewinner and then mated it with one of his own best birds, on the assumption that two such high-quality pigeons *simply must* produce very superior young. But often the youngsters' quality is disappointing, revealing weaknesses which were not visible in either parent: inherited, hidden features now emphasized in the offspring.

A characteristic of the Frillback *(left)* is the curled feathers along the back and outer wing coverts. Pouter pigeons *(below)* are bred for their unusual form.

Some Essentials in Starting with Fancy Pigeons

The particular fancy breed which a novice selects for his start in the pigeon-raising hobby should preferably be one that is fairly prolific, one that will raise at least three or four pairs of youngsters to maturity during a given season. At the conclusion of it, he will have a nice little flock of promising young birds from which to select likely candidates for exhibition in the fall and winter shows, as well as for breeding the following season. Depending on the particular variety he keeps, many a topnotch fancier is content with raising two or three sets of good youngsters per year. At all times he wants only quality.

In the second place the beginner should decide whether he wants to breed so-called color pigeons, as, for example: Archangels, Gimpels, Ice Pigeons, Starlings, Larks, and others; so-called type (form) pigeons, such as Pouters, Fantails, Show Homers, Carriers, and others; or so-called

Fantails—these birds represent one of the oldest breeds of domestic pigeons.

flying and performing breeds, such as Tumblers, Rollers, and Tipplers. He should realize also that no single so-called fancy breed is raised exclusively for color of plumage, for form or type of body conformation, or for ability to fly high, long, or to somersault. Most breeds of fancy pigeons are appraised on the basis of a number of essential qualities, which include both color of plumage and type of body structure, as are, for instance, Modenas, Magpies, Lahores, and many more varieties.

Whether a beginner selects for his first fancy breed a variety predominantly raised for its color, its type, or its flying ability is purely a matter of personal preference. But in making his initial choice, he should carefully consider the probable difficulties involved in producing high-quality offspring, which are most likely to meet the majority of the exacting provisions of the breed's official standard. Undoubtedly, exhibiting pigeons in various local, state, and national shows is one of the most ex-

The Dun-laced Blondinette hen, a variety of Oriental Frill, displays a neck frill, feathered legs, and attractive coloring.

Pair of African Owl pigeons.

citing and enjoyable incentives to raising fancy pigeons—*fine-quality* fancy pigeons! However, if the beginner selects as his first variety a breed such as the Magpie, Oriental Frill, Carrier, Maltese, or Show Homer, the youngsters—often few—raised during the first few years of his hobby may not possess quality sufficient to meet the usually severe competition furnished by birds shown by other and long-experienced people, who have kept, and improved, this particular breed during a lifetime. And when a beginner fails to place any winning birds in a show, he often becomes discouraged and loses interest in his hobby.

For these and other valid reasons, I strongly suggest that the novice start his fascinating pastime with a fairly easy-to-raise popular variety, perhaps Show Kings, Giant Homers, or some kind of Pouter, or Modena—all of which are usually good producers and dependable feeders. At this point, I must not neglect to emphasize that in actual practice, no variety of fancy pigeon is easy to raise to all standard specifications—an important fact which the beginner will discover as soon as he places his best birds in any fair-sized show. Nevertheless, in raising one of the aforementioned or other popular breeds, the beginner may not have to concentrate on many qualities all at once. Thus, if he keeps White Kings, he can concentrate on body conformation and weight, since the color will largely take care of itself.

A beginner's selection of a fancy breed with which to start his hobby would depend also on whether he wants an active, lively pigeon, which flies about a good deal in the loft or out-of-doors; or a quiet, more or less inactive pigeon, which does almost no flying at all, such as a Giant Runt, a Trumpeter, or similar breed, which, being bred for weight or for heavy feathering on certain parts of its body, or both, stays practically all day long on the floor of the loft. If the beginner lives on the outskirts of town or in the country, where his birds can have liberty once a day or oftener, and if he enjoys seeing them in vigorous flight, perhaps also engaging in aerial acrobatics, then Flying Tumblers, Rollers, or Tipplers may suit him best.

Before making up his mind, the novice should by all means visit some fanciers' lofts to learn how certain breeds of pigeons act in their home surroundings, where their behavior is much more natural than in the show hall. During such visits, he can discuss the good points with the fancier and observe at firsthand how these pigeons are most advantageously kept and treated, how well they breed, and what special facilities, if any, they require to remain in good health and to produce satisfactorily for a number of years. He should not buy any birds on his first visit, but should call on certain fanciers several times in order to learn more and more about the breed or breeds kept. In other words, he should not let his initial enthusiasm, which is often overenthusiasm, decide the issue, only to be dissatisfied with his choice when this feeling has waned. Rather, a genuine interest in a given breed, soundly based on its attractive or unusual coloring, or type, or behavior, or flying ability, or several of these desirable factors, should determine his final choice. And, finally, what is very conducive to rendering his hobby truly enjoyable, educational, and permanent, is to start his fancy-pigeon keeping with but *one* breed, buying the highest possible quality of birds he can afford.

Assuredly, it costs no more to feed and to care for one or more pairs of first-rate birds than to maintain the same number of inferior birds. And it is infinitely more satisfying to raise valuable stock which is likely to compete on even terms with that of other fanciers in the show—truly fancy stock. When friends or visitors call to look at the beginner's birds, he can show them with justifiable

The Maltese pigeon developed in Italy. A large, tall bird, its neck and legs are quite long, while its body is short and compact.

Pigmy Pouter, a small version of the English Pouter. This breed is especially suitable for novice pigeon fanciers.

Crested Helmet.

pride, knowing full well that they possess a certain "class" not found in pigeons of ordinary quality. Finally, high-grade fancy pigeons are often worth considerable money; for this good reason, many a novice is likely to treasure them more eagerly and to care for them more conscientiously than he would pigeons cheap in price and low in quality. A truly fine fancy pigeon not only deserves, but usually gets, "fancy" treatment in the loft!

Should the beginner want a breed which is tame and trusting, then let him get some Pigmy Pouters. These slim, long-limbed birds come in many attractive colors, including white, black, yellow, blue, silver, red, and dun. They are active almost the whole day long, never too tired to make love, as they "dance" and swagger about with globes inflated, constantly courting and cooing. If the novice prefers a Flying Pouter, there is the Swing Pouter, very popular among European fanciers, also bred in many colors and quite easy to raise. This Pouter should have the freedom of outdoors once a day or oftener, so that he may circle and swing gracefully over his loft, now and then clapping his powerful wings joyously. Since the Swing Pouter is strictly a flying pigeon, he should be kept only where he can enjoy daily the unrestrained freedom of the outdoors. To coop up such an active flyer permanently in a small loft is to treat him wrongly.

If it is mainly colorful plumage which the beginner desires his fancy pigeons to have, he has a choice of a great number of varieties, whose plumage boast either single colors or a combination of colors. Of exquisite coloring, for example, is the dainty little Ice Pigeon, with its delicate lavender blue which suggests the lavender of blue ice. It belongs to the so-called German Toy Pigeons, which are bred principally for lovely color and accurate markings, and not so much for type or form. To these Toys also belong Swallows, Helmets, Shields, Starlings, Priests, and many other breeds, which for lack of space cannot be described here. Some of them, as, for instance, the Swallows, are squatty birds with exceptionally attractive, strongly-contrasting markings and long foot feathers, while others, such as the Starlings, are trim, clean-legged birds, steady breeders as well as faithful feeders.

Exceedingly attractive in coloration of plumage are the Oriental Frills: dainty, short-faced (i.e., short-beaked), round-headed little birds with sharp, distinctive markings that cannot fail to attract any lover of truly beautiful pigeons. Some of the subvarieties include Satinettes, Brunettes, Silverettes, and Blondinettes, each one displaying unique and superlative coloring. Needless to say, the propagation of outstanding Oriental Frills is an exacting art. Its practice presupposes an intimate knowledge of color breeding and inheritance; a nice appreciation of color values; and, above all, the investment of much time, patience, and perseverance, since Oriental

Fancy-pigeon breeder, exhibitor, and judge William Hague *(above)* sits amidst his various ribbons and trophies. Another breeder *(below)* prepares one of his Frillbacks for showing.

Yellow Lahore cock *(above)*. Blue barless (blue-winged) Archangel cock *(facing page, above)*. Blue white-barred Blondinette hen *(facing page, below)*.

Schietti Modena.

Frills of known quality cannot be raised in a short space of time.

The Fantail is often selected by beginners, owing to its quaint beauty and because it is one of the oldest breeds of domestic pigeons, and one always displayed at pigeon shows. A dainty, charming tip-toe dancer, with upright chest; the small head thrown back gracefully; the circular tail complete, with even, close-fitting feathers, the Fantail is a good breeder, but an awkward flyer. It comes in white, black, red, silver, and other colors. To rear fine

Fantails likely to put up a good show in the exhibition coop is a very satisfying, though by no means an easy pastime. It can be recommended highly to the novice having considerable time and patience, and especially a discriminating eye for dainty, distinctive *living* form and *living* beauty.

Modenas also make an excellent hobby for the beginner. These graceful little birds are popular with many fanciers year after year, as evidenced by their numerous show entries. They are tame, easy to handle, and fairly prolific. A well-rounded, "curvaceous" bird, with smooth head, broad breast, wide shoulders, short back and short, uptilted tail, the Modena is divided into several classes. The so-called Gazzi Modena is white, except that head, upper throat, wings, flights, and tail are blue, black, red, yellow, silver, or other color. The Schietti Modena, excepting the all-white variety, has a colored body; it is bred in blue, silver, black, red, yellow, and other colors. There are also subvarieties.

The aforementioned are but a very small group of the several hundred breeds of fancy pigeons, many of which the novice fancier can see by visiting local pigeon shows, which are usually held in the fall and winter months. Once he has evinced a sincere and lively liking for a certain breed, has thoroughly investigated its probable advantages to him, and has obtained dependable information concerning its maintenance and breeding requirements, he should purchase two or three mated pairs of high quality, not over three years old. Then he can begin in earnest to enjoy the wonderful hobby of breeding fancy pigeons and also to assume its pleasant responsibilities. There is never-ending fun and eminent satisfaction to be derived from keeping fine pigeons—if only they are kept right and bred right!

Racing pigeons are banded when they are young *(left)*. Bands are dated and numbered. The Blue-barred English Owl *(below)* was originally bred as a flying pigeon, then as an exhibition bird.

*The Exciting Sports
of Flying and
of Racing Pigeons*

Many novices, both young and not so young, like their pigeons to be up and about—in the air, where they are in their natural element. Little wonder, therefore, that Flying Tumblers, Rollers, and Tipplers are preferred breeds with thousands of enthusiastic fanciers in this country. They care but little for the exhibition qualities of their birds, so long as they perform in the air up to their expectations. It should be noted that many so-called Rollers are simply high-flying, performing Tumblers, the term *Roller* being applied loosely by the pigeon fanciers. These Tumblers often provide just as much fun for their keepers as do genuine Rollers.

Born with the incentive to somersault, Roller pigeons, once released from their loft, ascend rapidly into the sky, some of them flying so high as to become invisible to the naked eye. Their rolling, or "spinning," consists of a

This pigeon has returned to its loft.

series of backward somersaults, performed speedily for a considerable distance. The longer the roll, the greater the value of the bird, even though short "spinners" are found in many kits.

Rollers perform best on calm, clear days, when visibility is good, and when there is no strong wind to carry them off their usual course. These aerial clowns are flown in *kits*, which are groups of birds that have been trained together and that act like well-knit flying units in the air. In other words, all members of the kit stay together while flying, and they return together at the conclusion of their flight. It is an exhilarating sight to watch a performing kit of Rollers execute their rapid somersaults, an exercise for which they are usually released once a day before feeding time. Often only males, not breeders, are members of a trained kit.

One of the ancient breeds of stunt flyers is the Oriental Roller, with its pearl eyes, fairly long beak, drooping

Through the ages, and especially during wartime, Racing Homers have been known for their exceptional ability to carry important messages. Here several "messengers" have been set up in a U.S. Air Force portable combat loft.

Show Tippler, light mottled bronze hen *(above)*. This specimen is an exhibition bird, whereas the Peking Nasal-tufted Pigeon *(facing page, above)* and the Blue-barred white-flighted Racing Homer *(facing page, below)* perform well in the air: the former as an acrobat, the latter as an endurance flier.

wings, and long, high tail. It is bred in black, white, red, almond, yellow, and other colors. Popular with thousands of fanciers in this country is the so-called Birmingham Roller, which was developed in and about Birmingham, England. It is a trim little bird with shallow keel, fairly long, narrow body, and tightly-folded tail. It occurs in a wide variety of colors. In recent years, various strains of Rollers, often named after their developers, as Pensom, Whittingham, and others, have been widely advertised in the pigeon press. However, the strains do not differ much either in physical properties or in flying ability. The most satisfactory way to buy Rollers is for the novice to visit a nearby fancier and watch his kit in action, then select good performers if these are for sale; if not, he should try to get youngsters from the good performers. West-of-England Tumblers, also bred in different colors, are known mainly for their ability to fly high and long. Well-trained kits will stay "up in the clouds" often for hours at a time, returning to their loft at their keeper's signal, which may be a white Fantail placed conspicuously on top of their loft, a rattling of the feed can, or some other cue—all meaning "come home and get it!" Finally, there are so-called Parlor Tumblers, which somersault backwards on the ground; hence they are often called Ground, or House, Tumblers. Placed on a lawn or other soft ground, these small, gentle pigeons, at the snap of a finger or the clap of a hand, will turn one or more backward somersaults. Like most tumblers, they are raised in different colors.

The ability to "hang in the clouds" for many hours has been especially well developed in the Tippler, a long-flying Tumbler. It is a rather small pigeon, with broad chest, strong wings, and short, clean legs. This breed also occurs in various colors. Some Flying Tipplers—they are game birds—have set records of staying sixteen and more hours in the air. When flying kits are overtaken

Racing Homers are released from their baskets which have been neatly stacked in a pigeon van. These birds have been highly trained for racing competition.

Pigeons are gentle and will allow a certain amount of handling by their keeper.

When a pigeon is released in unfamiliar territory away from its loft or cage, it will find its way home. This ability to return home is known as homing instinct.

Pigeon lofts can be expensive and sumptuous like the one above (with an attached flight), or they can be simple and moderately priced like the remodeled chicken house below.

Some of the perching facilities available in a Racing Homer loft.

by sudden, severe winds or thunderstorms, they tend to lose their bearings and go astray.

In some sections of the country, fanciers keeping Tumblers, Rollers, or Tipplers have organized both junior and senior clubs, which stage extremely exciting flying competitions at the individual lofts. A team of judges makes the rounds of the competing lofts, where the owners release their kits to the keen enjoyment of assembled club members and other interested spectators. A carefully considered system of points, usually based on the kind, quality, and length of performance, serves as the basis for judging each kit's performance. Though kept principally for their flying ability, Tumblers, Rollers, and Tipplers enjoy considerable popularity also as exhibition birds and are judged according to well-defined standards.

The sport of flying homing pigeons in competition

Some pigeon breeds are especially adapted to flying and performing aerial tricks, such as the Schoeneberg Tumbler *(above)* and the Parlor Tumbler *(below)*. Other breeds, like the Racing Homer *(facing page)*, are trained for short- and long-distance races, with emphasis on speed and endurance.

over varying distances has been the favorite pastime of young and old fanciers for a great many years. The racing, or homing, pigeon should not be confused with the Carrier—a fancy breed, not raised for flying, but solely for exhibition. In other words, racing pigeons are not Carrier pigeons.

The Racing Homer is a medium-sized bird, with firm, compact body, powerful wings, and tight plumage. By virtue of its keen, far-seeing eye and its intense urge to home, this excellent, alert flyer will, when released away from its loft, wing its lofty way home, braving wind and weather and other dangers. So that the homer may fly its fastest in races, it is subjected to rigid, carefully regulated training, which ordinarily consists of daily releases from gradually increasing distances along the intended race course, so that the bird will become more and more familiar with these new surroundings and perhaps remember some characteristic landmarks as future guideposts leading ultimately to the home loft.

The so-called short races include distances ranging from 100, 200, and 300 miles, while the long races cover from 500 to as many as 1000 miles. Ordinarily, young birds are flown over the short distances, and old and tried flyers over the long distances. Accordingly, each season racing-pigeon clubs schedule so-called young-bird races and old-bird races.

Probably no two clubs follow the same race procedure. But usually, in preparation for a race, the members bring their birds to the club rooms, where they are properly crated and then shipped to the race point, there to be released simultaneously. The release time is then wired to club headquarters, which in turn informs the participating members. At each loft, an electric clock usually serves to record the band number as well as the exact time of arrival of each returning bird. Once a fancier has been notified of the exact time of release, he estimates his

Racing pigeons also show the variations that are important primarily in fancy pigeons. The bird above displays a checkered pattern on its wings, while the bird below exhibits a barring pattern.

Racing Homer lofts *(above)* are usually situated on high ground so that the birds can get a panoramic view of the surrounding countryside. When these youngsters *(facing page, above)* become adults, they will be trained to become part of a racing team, or kit. White Danzig Highflier *(facing page, below)*.

Holding a pigeon just before releasing it.

birds' probable time of homecoming in the light of their past performance. As this time approaches, he begins to wait and watch eagerly, frequently scanning the horizon. Since every split-second counts in the winning, he must slip the special race band off his bird's legs the moment it traps, then drop it at once into the sealed clock, thus officially recording the exact moment of his pigeon's arrival. At the conclusion of the race, the clocks are opened at club headquarters, the speed of each bird is painstakingly calculated, and its ranking in the race thus determined. This, roughly, is organized racing-pigeon procedure. Varying with the particular races flown, diplomas, trophies, and other more or less valuable prizes are awarded to the owners of winning birds. The longer the race course, the larger the number of birds entered for the race, and the greater the obstacles, (such as high mountain terrain, unfavorable weather, birds of prey, etc.), the more highly valued is a winning bird's performance.

Most assuredly, flying racing pigeons in competition is a dynamic sport for young and old. To achieve sucess in it presupposes a strain of well-bred and soundly-trained birds, an intimate knowledge of their individual accomplishments over short and over long distances, and a broad insight into modern pigeon-racing techniques. It is a most exhilarating sport for intelligent, fair-minded lovers of truly fine pigeon blood—a serious hobby, requiring for its permanent enjoyment years of faithful application of sound sense to a sympathetic understanding of pigeon behavior under trying conditions.

Racing Homers are bred mostly in blues, blue-checks, red, red-checks, blacks, and other, rather plain colors, which render the birds inconspicuous when they are aloft. However, there are notable strains also of white and of splashed Homers.

If the novice wishes to make a start with homing pigeons, he should obtain young birds, called squeakers, which have not flown outside of their loft, since old birds, when released at a new loft, will return to their old one. The youngsters he buys should preferably come from a winning loft, one occupied by a strain of birds bred for both stamina and flying intelligence. Such birds, if correctly handled, will adjust themselves quickly to their new loft. If the novice wishes to enter some of his birds in races, he should join a local club, preferably one offering junior memberships. At its meetings he will learn, among other things, what is required to breed and to train racing pigeons, and also what is required to become a mature, intelligent, and fair-minded fancier. All in all, the sport of flying Racing Homers is a dramatic pastime—one that he can follow for many fruitful and most enjoyable years.

Nothing could be more exciting than to release one's pigeon *(left)* and watch it take flight with its powerful wings! All baby pigeons are called squabs (below); however, a squab is not ready for market until it is fully feathered.

Raising Utility, or Squabbing, Pigeons

Among pigeon men and women the term *utility pigeons* refers to those breeds which are kept to raise squabs either for the keeper's own use or for the commercial market, or both. These breeds include White Kings, Silver Kings, Giant Homers, Mondains, Carneaux, and various crosses of these and other varieties. Since they are meat producers of the first order, their squabs at marketing time, when they are about four weeks old, may weigh from half-a-pound to a pound and a pound-and-a-quarter apiece. Squab meat, usually tender and tasty and often regarded as a delicacy to be served on special occasions, ordinarily commands a substantial price in the market, where it seems to be in a class by itself. At any rate, it has never, and is not likely to, become a commonplace dish, because the demand for it is more or less limited. In this respect it is wholly unlike chicken.

When raised solely for meat production, Kings, Giant Homers, Mondains, Carneaux, and other breeds are not subject to any official standard. Their worth to the keeper is determined by the number, weight, and quality of the squabs they rear during the year. From five to seven, or even eight, pairs of young may be expected from a single pair of prolific utility pigeons. While fancy and various flying and performing pigeons are often rested during the winter months, with males and females separated, such is not the case with squabbing pigeons. They are kept working the year 'round. The exact length of their productive life varies with climatic conditions, their care, their inheritance, and some other factors not always under the control of their keeper.

Rarely are utility pigeons given the care and consideration bestowed on fancy or performing breeds. Especially where mass-production policies are applied to wrest every last ounce of squab meat from the old birds, as at squab farms, twenty or more pairs may be crowded into each of the numerous pens; and these are but rarely cleaned. They are, however, sprayed occasionally to destroy flies, lice, mites, and other pests whose presence in large numbers tends to lower the birds' production. On some pigeon farms, the birds are kept on wire in batteries. Such keeping facilitates control of each pair, and thus enables the keeper to cull poor producers promptly. Operators of such farms buy the various grains that make up the pigeons' feed mixture, or else buy the pellets, as well as the grit, in enormous quantities at the lowest possible prices. And to reduce their labor costs, many install automatic feeders, drinkers, and grain conveyors, usually operated by electricity.

Whether the novice squab producer plans his future operations to be limited or extensive, he will find a visit to a commercial squab plant extremely instructive and helpful. If he intends to enter the squab market on a considerable scale, he will need a very substantial amount of capital, sound business know-how, and lots of common sense to compete on favorable terms with existing squab producers. Such a venture involves more serious risks than are ordinarily encountered in starting more commonplace businesses. To raise numbers of plump, marketable squabs is not a difficult process, but to place them on the right market at the most propitious time, and sell them promptly and profitably is an entirely different and often a very tough proposition.

In conclusion, I want to emphasize the fact that the so-called utility breeds named are bred also for exhibition purposes. Thus, we have Show Kings, Show Carneaux, etc., each variety being bred to meet its own official exhibition standard. And it should not be forgotten that there are vast differences, for instances, between the appearance, stamina, and prolificacy of a Utility King and a Show King, which fact is not at all surprising, considering the wholly different reasons for which the two distinct classes of pigeons are kept.

PIGEONS